# KEYSTONES for READING

## COMPREHENSION ■ VOCABULARY ■ STUDY SKILLS

### Level A

Alden J. Moe, Ph.D.
*Lehigh University*

Sandra S. Dahl, Ph.D.
*University of Wisconsin*

Carol J. Hopkins, Ph.D.
*Purdue University*

John W. Miller, Ph.D.
*Georgia Southern College*

Elayne Ackerman Moe, M.Ed.
*Carbon-Lehigh Intermediate Unit*

MODERN CURRICULUM PRESS
Cleveland ● Toronto

# Table of Contents

# Words That Belong Together

Have you ever put silverware away? You may have sorted it into groups—knives, forks, and spoons.

Words can be put into groups, too. Look at the picture. Read the words in each group. Tell why they go together.

 ## KEYS to Grouping

### How are words alike?

**DIRECTIONS** Read each word in the box. Print its number on the correct line.

| | |
|---|---|
| 1. hair | 7. nose |
| 2. mouth | 8. ear |
| 3. knee | 9. eye |
| 4. finger | 10. head |
| 5. neck | 11. leg |
| 6. arm | 12. toe |

**DIRECTIONS** Circle the best name for this group of words.

Kinds of Toys        Parts of the Body        Things to Wear

## 2 Practice Grouping

**DIRECTIONS** Find the best word in the box for each sentence. Print it on the line.

| eat | pairs | run | head | arm |

_____

1. My nose, ears, and mouth are all on my _____ .

_____

2. My legs, knees, and feet all help me to _____ .

_____

3. My fingers and elbows are parts of my _____ .

_____

4. My mouth, teeth, and tongue all help me to _____ .

_____

5. My eyes, ears, and hands are all found in _____ .

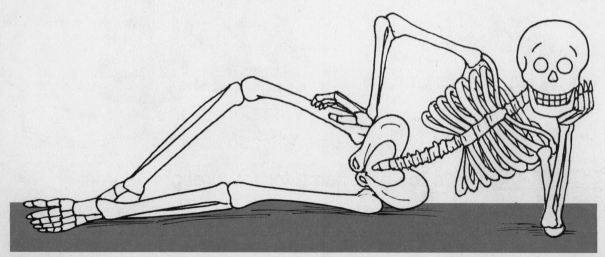

## 3 Read and Apply

**DIRECTIONS** Read the poem. Draw a line under each word that names a body part.

# Cat

The black cat yawns,
Opens her jaws,
Stretches her legs,
And shows her claws.

Then she gets up
And stands on four
Long stiff legs
And yawns some more.

She shows her sharp teeth.
She stretches her lip.
Her slice of a tongue
Turns up at the tip.

Lifting herself
On her delicate toes,
She arches her back
As high as it goes.

She lets herself down
With particular care,
And pads away
With her tail in the air.

—Mary Britton Miller

**DIRECTIONS** Read the words in the box. Can you put each word in the right group? Print each word on the correct line.

| | | | | | |
|---|---|---|---|---|---|
| bike | legs | car | toes | kite | butterfly |
| bird | skate | jet | tongue | tail | wagon |

## Group 1 Body Parts

_____    _____

_____    _____

_____    _____

## Group 2 Things That Fly

_____    _____

_____    _____

_____    _____

## Group 3 Things With Wheels

_____    _____

_____    _____

_____    _____

**REMEMBER** Think about what words have in common.

# Sticks, Stones, and Dragon Bones

Lesson **2**

"Sticks and stones may break my bones, but names will never hurt me."

Have you ever said that? In this lesson, you will learn about names. You will learn words that name people, places, and things. You will also meet a friendly dragon named Zack.

 **KEYS to Nouns**

**People. Places. Things.**

Some words are called nouns. They name people, places, and things.

| EXAMPLE | **José** is the name of a **person.** |
| | **School** is the name of a **place.** |
| | **Book** is the name of a **thing.** |

**DIRECTIONS** Read the words in the box. Each word is a noun. Find a picture of each word. Color each picture you find.

| tree | teacher | nut | pencil | clock |
| door | squirrel | bell | Carla | desk |

Nouns **5**

##  2  Practice With Nouns

**DIRECTIONS** Read each sentence. Read the words beside the sentence. Circle the noun.

1. John likes his new bike.          John          likes
2. Sing this song with me.          this          song
3. I go to school on Monday.          to          school

##  3  Read and Apply

**DIRECTIONS** Read the story about Zack the dragon. Draw Zack in the picture. The nouns in dark print can help you.

This is **Zack. Zack** is a **dragon.** He has many tiny **teeth.** His **wings** are purple. **Fire** comes out of his **mouth. Zack's** long green **tail** has **bumps** on it. He has four **legs.** Each **foot** has four **toes.**

**Zack** likes **children.** He also likes **popcorn. Zack** helps the **children.** How does he help them?

**REMEMBER** Nouns name people, places, and things.

**6** Nouns

# Words That Tell What We Can Do

You can be proud of things you can do. Maybe you can skate, ride a bike, run fast, draw a picture, or read a book.

In this lesson, you will learn about words that tell what we can do. These words are called verbs. You will read a funny poem with unusual verbs.

 ## KEYS to Verbs

**Find the action words.**

DIRECTIONS Read the words in the box. They are all verbs. Choose one verb to act out. Have a friend guess which verb you chose.

| | | | | |
|---|---|---|---|---|
| run | fly | sing | jump | dance |
| see | hop | pull | skip | read |

 ## 2  Practice With Verbs

DIRECTIONS Here is a list of jobs to do. Read each sentence. Look at the words beside the sentence. Circle the verb.

1. Clean your room.     clean     room
2. Feed the cat.     feed     cat
3. Take out the trash.     trash     take
4. Eat your lunch.     your     eat
5. Play with Shane.     play     Shane

# Sulk

I scuff
   my feet along
And puff
   my lower lip
I sip my milk
   in slurps
And huff
And frown
And stamp around
And tip my chair
   back from the table
Nearly fall down
   but I don't care
I scuff
And puff
And frown
And huff
And stamp
And pout
Till I forget
What it's about

      —Felice Holman

# Changing Places

Different people use different words to talk about you. Your parents call you "son" or "daughter." Your classmates call you "friend." All those words mean <u>you</u>.

In this lesson, you will learn about words that can change places with other words.

## KEYS to Pronouns

**Pronouns replace nouns.**

**LEARN** Pronouns are words like <u>I</u>, <u>they</u>, <u>he</u>, <u>she</u>, or <u>it</u>. They can take the place of naming words, or nouns. Without pronouns, you would read the same word over and over.

**EXAMPLE** Without pronouns: Mary and Harry like to ride Mary's and Harry's bikes.

With pronoun: Mary and Harry like to ride **their** bikes.

**DIRECTIONS** Read each sentence. Circle the pronoun that can change places with the underlined words.

1. <u>Virgil</u> is a good player.        He        Them        She
2. <u>Jan and Jack</u> are twins.         I         You         They
3. Mom threw <u>the ball</u> to Pat.      we        it          me

Pronouns **9**

**Practice With Pronouns**

DIRECTIONS Read each pair of sentences. Find the underlined pronoun. Circle the word or words in the first sentence that the pronoun replaces.

**1.** Tab and Sam are kittens. They want to play with the toy.

**2.** The play was funny. The class liked it.

## 3 Read and Apply

DIRECTIONS Read the story. Then read the sentences. Circle the word the underlined pronoun can replace.

"Get up!" Mom called.

Lisa jumped out of bed. She knew why Mom was calling. She raced to the barn.

Daddy was there. He pointed to the new colt. It had a white patch between its eyes.

"Let's call it Star," Lisa whispered.

The colt's mother took good care of her baby. She licked it clean. She gave it milk.

"Let's go now," said Daddy. "The new baby needs its rest."

**1.** She raced to the barn.

    Mom        Dolly        Lisa

**2.** It had a white patch.

    colt        Daddy        Lisa

REMEMBER Pronouns replace nouns.

# Hide and Seek Treasure

Lesson
**5**

Do you ever play Hide and Seek? Where do you hide?
Do you hide in a tree, behind a bush, or under a bed?
Words like <u>in</u>, <u>behind</u>, and <u>under</u> tell where to look.

In this lesson, you will look for a hidden treasure. Words
that tell where will help you.

 **KEYS to Words That Tell Where**

**Where can you look?**

**LEARN** Read the words that tell where.

| above | on | in | under | up | beside |
|-------|-----|-----|-------|-----|--------|

**DIRECTIONS** Find each small picture in the big picture. Put its
letter beside the words that tell where you found it.

**A.**

**B.**

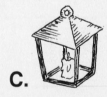

**C.**

_____ above the table       _____ on his head       _____ in a box

Prepositions Prepositions **11**

# Practice With Words That Tell Where

**DIRECTIONS** Print the correct word on the line under each picture.

| over behind between in under around up down beside |

_____

_____

<br>

_____

_____

_____

_____

_____

_____

<br>

_____

_____

_____

_____

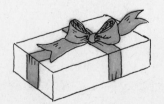

_____

_____

<br>

_____

_____

_____

_____

## 3 Read and Apply

**DIRECTIONS** Read the story about a pirate's secret. Draw a line to show the path Captain Max took. (Words that tell where can help you.) Put an X on the secret hiding place.

Captain Max dragged his old pirate chest from the cave. He carried it to Turtle Rock. He hid behind the rock. He looked around. Then he sneaked to the stream.

Captain Max crossed the stream. He stepped on stones in the water. He ran between the twin trees. No one saw him. Then he pulled his treasure up the hill.

His boat was in the bay. Captain Max rowed it to his ship, the Sea Dragon. His crew was asleep. He was glad. Someday he would come back. He would hide new treasure in his secret cave.

Read the poem about a turtle. Answer each
question with a word group that tells where.

There was a little turtle.
He lived in a box.
He swam in a puddle.
He climbed on the rocks.

He snapped at a mosquito.
He snapped at a flea.
He snapped at a minnow.
He snapped at me.

He caught the mosquito.
He caught the flea.
He caught the minnow,
But he didn't catch me.

—Vachel Lindsay

_____

- - - - - - - - - - - - - - - - - - - - -

**1.** Where did the turtle live? _____

_____

- - - - - - - - - - - - - - - - - - - - -

**2.** Where did the turtle swim? _____

_____

- - - - - - - - - - - - - - - - - - - - -

**3.** Where did the turtle climb? _____

Some words tell where.

# It's All the Same to Me!

Miss Muffet was afraid of spiders. When she saw one, she probably screamed. You could also say she yelled, shouted, or screeched.

In this lesson, you will learn words that mean almost the same thing. You will get to know Miss Muffet again.

## 1 KEYS to Synonyms

**Synonyms have almost the same meanings.**

**LEARN** Words with the same meaning are **synonyms. Scream** and **shout** are synonyms. So are **happy** and **glad.**

**DIRECTIONS** Circle the two synonyms in each group of words.

**1.** little    big    small          **2.** jog    sit    run

## 2 Practice With Synonyms

**DIRECTIONS** Read the first sentence in each pair. Print the synonym for the underlined word on the line.

**1.** The red ball is <u>little</u>. The red ball is _____.

**2.** Mom can <u>jog</u> two miles. Mom can _____ two miles.

## 3   Read and Apply

**DIRECTIONS** Read the poem. It sounds funny, doesn't it? Fix it by using a synonym for each underlined word. Use the words in the box. Print the new poem on the lines.

<u>Small</u> Miss Muffet sat on her <u>stool</u>
<u>Chewing</u> her <u>cottage cheese</u>.
Along came a spider
Who sat down <u>next to</u> her
And <u>scared</u> Miss Muffet <u>gone</u>.

| beside | tuffet | away | Little | frightened |
|---|---|---|---|---|
| | Eating | curds and whey | | |

_____                        _____
- - - - - - - - - -                              - - - - - - - - - - - - -
_____ Miss Muffet sat on her _____
_____   _____
- - - - - - - - - -       - - - - - - - - - - - - -
_____ her _____.

Along came a spider
              _____
              - - - - - - - - - -

Who sat down _____ her
_____              _____
- - - - - - - - - -                   - - - - - - - - - - - -
And _____ Miss Muffet _____.

**REMEMBER** Synonyms mean almost the same thing.

# Eight Ate Cake for Four

Does the name of this lesson make sense? It does, if you think of the meaning of each word and not just the sound.

In this lesson, you will learn the meanings of some tricky words. You will also go to a party.

## KEYS to Homonyms

**Different words can sound the same.**

**LEARN** Some words sound the same, but have different meanings. These words are called homonyms.

**EXAMPLE** **Ate** and **eight** are homonyms. They sound the same. They mean different things. **Ate** means "swallowed food." **Eight** is a number.

**DIRECTIONS** Draw a line under the homonyms in each pair of sentences. Tell what each homonym means.

1. I ate three cookies.

2. Libby is eight years old.

3. Grandpa sent me a gift.

4. The gum cost one cent.

5. My nose is on my face.

6. She knows my name.

7. The flower is red and pink.

8. We need flour to make a cake.

**Practice With Homonyms**

**DIRECTIONS** Read the homonyms in the box. Find the word that names each picture. Print it on the line under the picture. Look back at page 17 for help with meanings.

| | | | | | |
|---|---|---|---|---|---|
| ate | bear | flower | nose | cent | blew |
| eight | bare | flour | knows | sent | blue |

## 3 Read and Apply

**DIRECTIONS** Read the story. Find a word in the box with the same meaning as each picture. Print the word on the correct line.

| eight | nose | blue | bear |
|-------|------|------|------|
| ate | knows | blew | bare |

Carlos made a birthday wish. There were **1.**

candles on his cake. Carlos **2.**  them all out.

Just before everyone **3.**  the cake, Grandma and Grandpa came. Carlos saw Grandpa's coat pocket wiggle.

Then he saw a little wet **4.**  and two tiny paws.

"Look out!" yelled Grandpa. "I have a **5.**  in my pocket!"

"No, you don't," said Carlos. "You have a puppy. Is it for me?"

_____    _____    _____

- - - - - - - - -    - - - - - - - - -    - - - - - - - - -

**1.** _____    **2.** _____    **3.** _____

- - - - - - - - -    - - - - - - - - -

**4.** _____    **5.** _____

Read each sentence. Circle the correct homonym.

1. Carlos' puppy is only _____ weeks old.  ate    eight

2. It looks like a fuzzy _____ cub.  bear    bare

3. It _____ its name is Pepper.  knows    nose

4. It has a new _____ collar.  blew    blue

5. The puppy likes to play in Dad's _____.  flours    flowers

6. It likes to chase Carlos' _____ feet.  bear    bare

7. One day Pepper _____ Sis's slipper.  ate    eight

8. Carlos _____ Pepper to bed for that!  cent    sent

9. Then he spent ten _____ for a dog toy.  cents    sents

10. A big wind _____ in the kitchen window.  blew    blue

11. Pancake _____ spilled on the floor.  flour    flower

12. Of course, the pup poked its ___ in it.  knows    nose

REMEMBER Homonyms sound the same but have different meanings.

# Follow the Leader

**When you play Follow the Leader, the leader shows you what to do. When you do school work, the directions tell you what to do.**

**In this lesson, you will learn how directions can help you. You will read a poem that gives directions.**

 **1** **KEYS to Following Directions**

### Read! Look! Listen!

**DIRECTIONS** Learn the direction words in the box.

| | | | | | |
|---|---|---|---|---|---|
| draw | find | picture | under | circle | line |
| print | around | sentence | look | read | on |

 **2** **Practice Following Directions**

**1.** Draw a line under the word <u>cat</u>.　　　　　　　cat

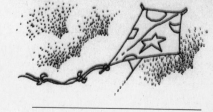

**2.** Circle the kite.

_ _ _ _ _ _ _ _ _

**3.** Print your name on the line.　　　　　　_ _ _ _ _ _ _ _ .

DIRECTIONS Play a game with the poem below. Act out the directions while someone reads the poem aloud.

## Hands Up

Reach for the ceiling,
Touch the floor,
Stand up again.
Let's do more.

Touch your head,
Then your knee,
Up to your shoulder,
Like this, see.

Reach for the ceiling,
Touch the floor.
That's all now.
There isn't any more.

REMEMBER Following directions saves time and trouble.

# You Said It!

**Cows say, "Moo." Ducks quack. People talk. In this lesson, you will learn to tell who is talking when you read.**

##  KEYS to Finding the Speaker

**Look for the clues.**

**LEARN**  1. Look for these marks: " ". The words in between are being spoken aloud.
2. Look for groups of words like these: <u>said Joan</u>, <u>Mr. Jones shouted</u>, <u>Bob asked</u>. They let you know who is speaking.

**DIRECTIONS** Put a check on the line if someone is speaking.

_____ 1. "Throw me the ball!" yelled Sandy.
_____ 2. The dog caught the ball.
_____ 3. "That was funny," laughed Dad.

## ② Practice Finding Spoken Words

**DIRECTIONS** Draw a line under the words that are being said aloud. Circle the name of the person who said them.

1. "The party is a surprise," whispered Ivy.

2. "Here, Boomer," yelled Jeff.

3. "Let's go to the park," said Mother.

Understanding Dialogue **23**

"Look out!" shouted Ruthie. "You will run into my dog!"

"Oh, no!" Alan cried.

Alan turned his bike. He just missed Ruthie's dog. Then he fell down.

Ruthie looked scared. Ruthie's dog looked scared. Alan started to cry.

"I didn't mean to run into your dog," he sobbed.

"You didn't run into my dog," said Ruthie. "You missed him when you fell. The dog is fine. Are you?"

Alan stopped crying. He started to laugh.

"I will be a better driver," he said. "I will watch where I am going. I scared the dog, and I scared myself."

**1.** Who said, "Look out"? _____

**2.** Who said, "The dog is fine"? _____

**3.** Who said, "I will be a better driver"? _____

**REMEMBER** Look for " " and for words that mean <u>said</u>.

# Getting It Right

Have you ever baked a cake? You have to do everything just right. If you forget something, you could make a mess.

In this lesson, you will learn to get things right when you read. You will read about an animal that looks like a giant teddy bear—the panda.

##  KEYS to Remembering Details

### Reading is remembering.

**LEARN** Think about what you read. Be sure you understand each part before you go on. Ask yourself questions about what you read.

**DIRECTIONS** Read the story. Circle the correct answers.

Janet and Cathy went to the zoo with their class. They saw many different animals. Some children liked the monkeys best. Some liked the tigers. Janet and Cathy liked the bears.

1. Where did Janet and Cathy go?
   to the park      to the store      to the zoo

2. Which animals did Janet and Cathy like best?
   monkeys      tigers      bears      chickens

# ② Practice Remembering Details

**DIRECTIONS** Read the story. Answer the questions. Then color the poster.

Janet and Cathy looked at all the bears.

"I like the black and white bear best," said Cathy. "It is so cute."

"That is a very special animal," said the zookeeper. "It looks like a bear, but it is a giant panda. Pandas come from China. It is hard for them to find food. We must take good care of pandas. If we don't, all pandas may be gone someday."

That made the girls sad. They wanted to help. When they went back to school, they made a surprise for the class. Look at their surprise. It is a poster.

1. What are the black and white animals called?

_____
_ _ _ _ _ _
_____
_____
_ _ _ _ _ _

2. Where do pandas come from?

_____
_____
_ _ _ _ _ _

3. What was Janet and Cathy's surprise?

_____

**26** Noting Details

## 3 Read and Apply

**DIRECTIONS** Read the story. Remember the details.

That night Janet and her big brother did their homework together.

"Bill," said Janet. "I have to write a story about my favorite animal. How can I find out about pandas?"

"I'll help you," said Bill. "We'll look in the encyclopedia."

Janet and Bill looked up panda. Bill read to Janet.

Giant pandas are large black and white animals. They look like bears. Pandas can grow to be 5 feet (1.5 meters) tall. They can weigh 300 pounds (140 kilograms).

Giant pandas live in China and Tibet. They live on mountains. Pandas eat plants called bamboo. They need to live in bamboo forests.

Wild pandas are in trouble. There are fewer and fewer bamboo forests. Pandas have less room to live. They have less food to eat. Pandas are becoming very rare.

Even though pandas look like bears, most scientists say they are not. They say pandas are in the raccoon family.

"Thanks, Bill," said Janet. "Now I know just what to write."

Noting Details **27**

black  bamboo  pandas  bears  China  help  white  raccoons

## My Favorite Animal

I like _____ best.
They are _____ and
_____. They look
like _____. They
are more like _____.
Pandas live in _____.
They eat _____.
Pandas need our _____.

# First Things First

**What if you put on your coat before your shirt? That would be silly. The right order is important.**

**The right order is important in a story, too. In this lesson, you will learn how order makes a story make sense.**

 ## KEYS to Words That Show Order
### First. Next. Last.

**LEARN** Learn the words in the box.

| next | last | then | after | before | first |
|------|------|------|-------|--------|-------|

**DIRECTIONS** Circle the word that shows order.

1. First we went to the lake.

2. Dad took a nap after lunch.

3. We will ride the train next.

4. Then it started to rain.

 ## Practice With Words That Show Order

**DIRECTIONS** The pictures below tell a story. The story is not in order. Make the story make sense. Print 1, 2, 3, or 4 in the box in the corner of each picture.

DIRECTIONS Read all the sentences. Number the sentences to put them in order. Write the story on the lines.

_____ Next it took him to the sea.

_____ Roy dreamed his toy train could fly.

_____ At last, it took him back to his own bed.

_____ First it took him to a big city.

_____

_____

_____

_____

_____

_____

_____

_____

REMEMBER Look for words that show order.

# Picture This

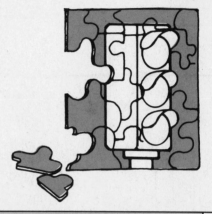

It's fun to put puzzles together.
Each part is a piece of the whole
picture. Some stories have pictures.
The pictures are like puzzle pieces.

In this lesson, you will learn to
put words and pictures together to
understand a story.

 **KEYS to Picture Clues**
### Pictures tell a story.

**LEARN** When you read a story, look at the pictures, too.
They can help you figure out a hard word. They can tell things
that are not written in the words.

**DIRECTIONS** Circle the number of the sentence that tells about
the picture.

**A.**

1. The spider is making a web.

2. The spider is swinging in the air.

**B.**

1. The car will go now.

2. The car can not go.

**C.**

1. The white rabbit is big.

2. The white rabbit is little.

**D.**

1. It is time to go to bed.

2. It is time to eat lunch.

**Practice With Picture Clues**

**DIRECTIONS** Read the stories. Color the picture that goes with each story.

**1.** An octopus is a strange animal. It lives in the sea. It has eight arms. If one arm comes off, the octopus can grow a new one.

**2.** I can make my own lunch. I will make a sandwich. I will put milk in my thermos. Should I have an apple or a banana?

**3.** Sue has a pet. She takes care of it herself. She feeds her pet. She teaches it tricks. Sue and her pet play games. Sometimes they take a walk. Sue and her pet have fun.

## 3 Read and Apply

**DIRECTIONS** Read the stories. Look at the pictures. Then read the sentences. Print **T** on the line if the sentence is true. Print **F** if it is false.

**A.** Amy and her brother went on a picnic. Justin got the picnic basket. Amy made sandwiches. Justin filled a thermos with milk. Then they added some fruit.

   Amy and Justin took a blanket and walked to the creek. They spread the blanket under a tree. They had a nice lunch.

\_\_\_\_\_ **1.** Amy is younger than Justin.
\_\_\_\_\_ **2.** They took sandwiches.
\_\_\_\_\_ **3.** Their dog did not go with them.
\_\_\_\_\_ **4.** Some fruit is in the basket.

**B.** One day Chris brought home a kitten. Mom said it could stay if it was good. Chris hugged the kitten. Chris called the kitten Tiger.

   Tiger was <u>not</u> good. She was always in trouble. Tiger knocked the plants over. She scratched the sofa. Mom said Tiger had to go.

   ''Tomorrow,'' she said, ''you must find a new home for Tiger.''

That night Tiger woke Mom. She jumped on her. She clawed the pillow. Then she tugged at the blanket. Mom was really mad.

"Out you go!" she told Tiger.

Mom picked Tiger up. She took her to the kitchen. When she got there, Mom forgot all about Tiger. She saw smoke. It was coming from the basement.

Mom woke Chris. Chris, Mom, and Tiger raced next door to call the fire department. They came and put out the fire.

"You were lucky," said the fire chief. "You found the fire in time. You were not hurt. Your house was not hurt much."

Mom hugged Tiger.

"Thank you, Tiger," she said. "You saved our lives. You are a hero. You can stay forever."

_____ 1. Chris called the kitten Spot.
_____ 2. Tiger has stripes.
_____ 3. Tiger woke Mom.
_____ 4. Smoke came from the attic.
_____ 5. Chris is a girl.

**REMEMBER** Pictures work with words to tell a story.

# Riddles and More Riddles

Sometimes the words on the page don't tell you everything. You need to find clues to help you understand a story. Some clues are in the words. Some are in pictures. Some are already in your head.

In this lesson, you will learn to use clues to make good guesses about what you read.

## KEYS to Making Good Guesses

**Read. Think. Make a good guess.**

**LEARN** Use clues from the pictures and clues in the words. Use what you already know. Think about what you read.

**DIRECTIONS** Look at each picture. Read the sentence below it. Circle YES or NO.

We will eat lunch soon.

YES  NO

The baby will smile now.

YES  NO

**2 Practice Making Good Guesses**

**DIRECTIONS** Read the first sentence in each group. Circle the letter of the sentence that comes next.

1. The tire was flat.

   a. Mom changed the tire.

   b. We drove to the beach.

2. It was raining.

   a. We played in the yard.

   b. We put a puzzle together.

3. The door bell rang.

   a. I drank my milk.

   b. Dad went to the door.

4. Miss White is our teacher.

   a. She reads aloud to us.

   b. The fuzzy cat is white.

**DIRECTIONS** Read the story. Make a good guess. Circle yes or no. Then circle the words in the story that were your clues. Draw a picture of David and Jenny.

David put on his new blue mittens. Then he got his sled. He went to the park to play. At the park, he met Jenny. She wore boots and a warm, green coat. They played with the sled. The time went fast. Soon it was time to go home.

1. Did they play in the park on a hot, summer day?    yes    no

## 3 Read and Apply

**DIRECTIONS** Look at the picture. Read the story. Then circle the answer to each question.

The Biddle family will have fun. The little Biddles put bats and balls into the van. Mr. Biddle puts toys in, too. The toys can go in the water. Here comes Mrs. Biddle with something good to eat. What a good day they will have!

| | | |
|---|---|---|
| 1. Mr. Biddle is going to work. | True | False |
| 2. The Biddles will play baseball. | True | False |
| 3. They will go swimming. | True | False |
| 4. Mother feels very sad. | True | False |
| 5. The Biddles will have a picnic. | True | False |
| 6. They are going on an airplane. | True | False |
| 7. Father will be mad if the toys get wet. | True | False |
| 8. The little Biddles do not want to go. | True | False |

Read the riddles. Each sentence has a clue. Put the letter of the right picture on the line in front of each riddle.

_____ 1. I like to eat oats.
I can gallop and trot.

A.

_____ 2. I am red, yellow, and green.
I tell you to stop, wait, and go.

B.

_____ 3. I am fun to ride at the fair.
I go round and round.

C.

_____ 4. I can jump.
I like to live near a pond.

D.

_____ 5. I stay on a shelf.
You can read me.

E.

**DIRECTIONS** Follow the dots. Find the answer to the riddle.

I have eyes, but can not see.
I come from the ground.
What can I be?

Color me brown.

**REMEMBER** Use clues from the page and clues from your head.

**38** Making Inferences

# What Next?

It's fun to listen while someone tells stories. It's even more fun to try to guess what will happen next. The same thing is true when you read.

In this lesson, you will learn to think ahead when you read. You will learn to guess what will happen next.

 ## KEYS to Thinking Ahead

### What will happen next?

**LEARN** When you read, think about what has already happened. Think of all the different things that could happen next. Make your best guess.

**DIRECTIONS** Look at pictures A and B. Think about what has happened. Color the picture that will finish the story.

**A**

**B**

DIRECTIONS Read the stories. Look at the pictures. Find the picture that shows the end of each story. Print its letter on the line.

_____ **1.** Bev got some colored paper. She made her bike look pretty. Then she rode to the park. Other children were already there. They all wanted to be in the contest.

_____ **2.** Timmy could not find his little brother. He looked in the yard. He looked in the house. He called and called. Then Timmy had an idea. He knew it was time for Eddie's nap.

_____ **3.** Stacy pushed the little man down into the box. She turned the handle. Stacy and her cousin heard the music. Then they heard a soft click.

A            B            C

## 3 Read and Apply

**DIRECTIONS** Read the story. Draw a picture to show how you think the story will end.

Hannah's mother gave her a red balloon. It was on a long string. Hannah held tight to the string. She took her balloon for a walk in the yard.

Hannah liked to walk along with her big red balloon. Hannah waited for her brother Jeff to come home. She wanted to show him the balloon.

Jeff was coming home from school. He could see Hannah playing in the yard. He saw the big red balloon. Just then a big gust of wind blew by. It blew the balloon away from Hannah.

Hannah started to cry. The balloon went up and up and away. Jeff started to run. He was too late. The balloon was going up into the tree.

How do you think the story will end? Draw a picture to show your ending.

Now turn the page to read the author's ending.

The balloon went up and up. It went into a tree. It was stuck on a branch. Jeff climbed up into the tree. He reached for the string. Then he climbed down slowly. He was afraid the balloon would break.

Soon Jeff was back on the ground. The big red balloon was still big and red and round. Jeff gave the balloon back to his little sister.

Hannah gave Jeff something, too. She gave him a big hug!

**REMEMBER** If your ending is something that could have happened, it was a good guess.

# Peanut Butter and Pickles

Are peanut butter and pickles alike or different? They look different. They taste different. They are alike in at least one way. You can eat both.

In this lesson, you will learn to think about how things are alike and different.

 **KEYS to Comparing**

How are things alike? How are they different?

**LEARN** When you think about how things are alike or different, you compare them. There are many ways to compare.

**DIRECTIONS** Look at the pictures in each box. Read the words under the box. If the pictures are alike in the way the word says, print **A** on the line. If they are different, print **D**.

_____ size _____ shape _____ color

 **Practice Comparing**

**DIRECTIONS** Read the questions. Circle the answers.

1. Which things are animals?          elephant  mouse  box  wagon
2. Which ones can you carry
   things in?                         elephant  mouse  box  wagon

# 3 Read and Apply

DIRECTIONS Which picture is different? Put an X on the picture that does not belong in each group.

1.

2.

3.

DIRECTIONS Which things are alike? Color the pictures that belong in each group.

1.

2.

3.

REMEMBER Think about how things are alike.

# Let's Get Organized

If you had to write the alphabet, where would you start? It's easy when you put the letters in order.

In this lesson, you will learn ways to put things in order. That will make them easier to remember.

## 1 KEYS to Organizing

**Organizing helps you remember.**

**LEARN** When you put things in order, you organize them.

**DIRECTIONS** Draw a picture of an ant, an elephant, and a cat. Draw them in order from smallest to largest.

| | | |
|---|---|---|
| 1 | 2 | 3 |

## 2 Practice Organizing

**DIRECTIONS** Now organize another way. Print the names of the three animals. Print the largest on the first line.

_____   _____   _____

1. _____   2. _____   3. _____

# 3 Read and Apply

**DIRECTIONS** Read the story. Number the events. Print them in order on the lines.

Luis was busy after school. He changed his clothes. Then he ran outside to find his friend Eddie. They played until it was time for dinner.

After dinner, Luis did his homework. It felt good to have it all done. Luis still had time to watch his favorite TV show. By then, Luis was tired. He had had a busy day. He was ready to go to sleep.

__ sleep     __ watch TV     __ play

__ eat     __ do homework

_____          _____

1. _____          4. _____

2. _____          5. _____

3. _____

Test yourself. Close your eyes. Try to remember the events in the story.

**REMEMBER** Things make sense when they are organized.

# Off to the Right Start

Can you make a model or tie your shoe? Then you know it's important to get each step right. It's just as important to know when to do each step.

In this lesson, you will put steps in the right order.

## ⚠️ 1 KEYS to Putting Steps in Order

**Know what to do. Know when to do it.**

**LEARN** When you follow directions, think about all the things you need to do. Then think about when to do them.

**DIRECTIONS** Read the sentences. Put 1 on the line before the step you do first. Put 2 before the next step.

_____ Button the buttons.          _____ Put your arms in the sleeves.

## 2 Practice Putting Steps in Order

**DIRECTIONS** Which step comes first, second, third, and fourth. Put the correct number on the line in front of the sentence.

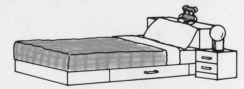

_____ Put the pillow on the bed.

_____ Put the sheets on the bed.

_____ Put the blanket on.

_____ Tuck the sheets under.

**DIRECTIONS** Number the sentences to show the correct order.

**Brushing Your Teeth**

_____ **A.** Put the toothpaste and brush away.

_____ **B.** Put water and toothpaste on the brush.

_____ **C.** Rinse your mouth with water.

_____ **D.** Brush carefully.

**Making a Sandwich**

_____ **A.** Put the other slice on top.

_____ **B.** Put peanut butter on one slice.

_____ **C.** Cut the sandwich in half.

_____ **D.** Take out two slices of bread.

**REMEMBER** What should you do? When should you do it?

# Now I Know

**What would you like to know more about? Do you like dinosaurs? Do you know how to build a kite? Reading can help you know more about things you like.**

**In this lesson, you will practice learning from what you read.**

 ## KEYS to Reading to Find Out

### Ask yourself questions. Read to find answers.

**LEARN** Before you read, think about what you already know. Think about what you want to know. Then read to find out.

**DIRECTIONS** Read the questions at the bottom of the page. Then read to find the answers. When you finish the story, answer the questions.

Garden snails move very slowly. They don't have to hurry. They have shells to protect them.

Different snails have different kinds of shells. The shapes can be different. So can the colors. When snails grow, their shells grow, too.

Mother snails lay their eggs in the ground. Soon the eggs hatch. The baby snails find green leaves to eat. They eat green leaves and grow.

Snails find a place to sleep in winter. They go into their shells and sleep until spring. Then they wake up. They find more leaves to eat.

1. Do all snails look alike?      YES      NO

2. Do snails lay eggs?      YES      NO

**DIRECTIONS** On the line below, write one question about spiders. Then read the story. Answer the questions at the end of the story.

Your
Question _____

Have you ever seen a cobweb? Cobwebs are made by spiders. Spiders can spin silk from their bodies. They use it to make webs. Spiders catch food in their webs. They like to catch flies, beetles, and ants.

The mother spider lays eggs. She wraps them in silk. When the babies hatch, their mother is gone. The babies are ready to live on their own.

There are many kinds of spiders. Some are big and hairy. Others are small. Most spiders won't hurt you. They just want to catch bugs and spin webs.

1. Did the story answer your question? _____

2. Write one thing you learned about spiders.

_____

_____

**DIRECTIONS** Now read about frogs and tadpoles. When you finish, turn the page and answer the questions.

Most babies look a lot like their parents. Baby frogs don't. Grown frogs have legs with big webbed feet. They can breathe on land. They don't have tails.

Baby frogs are called tadpoles. They look more like fish. They have legs. They have tails. They breathe in the water through gills.

The mother frog lays her eggs in the water. Then she goes away. At first, the eggs look like little balls of jelly. Each egg has a tiny dot inside. The dot is a tadpole. Tadpoles start to grow in the eggs.

Soon the tadpoles hatch from the eggs. They swim to a weed and hold on. The tadpoles eat the weed. They grow strong. Legs begin to grow. Their gills disappear. Their tails get smaller and smaller.

At last the tadpoles become frogs. They look just like their parents.

1. Which animals come from eggs?
   ○ **a.** only snails and spiders
   ○ **b.** only spiders and frogs
   ○ **c.** snails, spiders, and frogs

2. Which animals have shells?
   ○ **a.** snails
   ○ **b.** spiders
   ○ **c.** frogs

3. Which babies don't look like their parents?
   ○ **a.** snails
   ○ **b.** spiders
   ○ **c.** frogs

4. Which babies take care of themselves?
   ○ **a.** snails and spiders
   ○ **b.** spiders and frogs
   ○ **c.** snails, spiders, and frogs

5. Which babies look like fish?
   ○ **a.** snails
   ○ **b.** spiders
   ○ **c.** frogs

**REMEMBER** Question yourself. Read to find answers.

Over in the meadow,
in a sunny beehive,
Lived a mother bumblebee
and her little bees five.
"Buzz!" said the mother.
"We buzz," said the five.
So they buzzed and they hummed,
Near the sunny beehive.

O ver in the meadow,
        by an old
            barn door,
Lived an old mother rat
    and her little rats four.
"Gnaw!" said the mother.
"We gnaw," said the four.
So they gnawed and they chewed,
On the grain near the door.

7

Over in the meadow,
in a nest
    made of sticks,
Lived a black mother crow
and her little crows six.
"Caw!" said the mother.
"We caw," said the six.
So they cawed all day,
In their nest made of sticks.

6

12

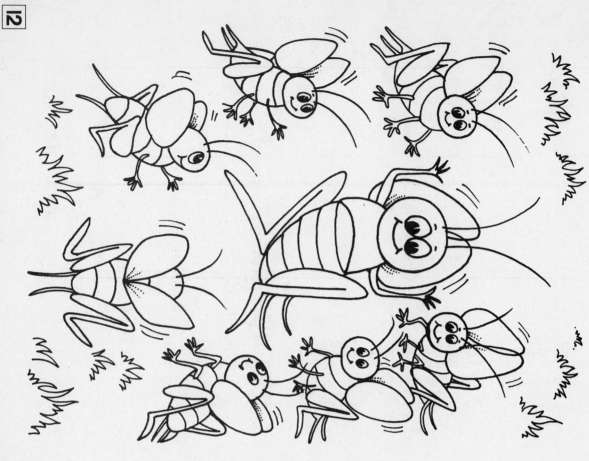

Over in the meadow,
in a hole
in the tree,
Lived an old mother owl
and her little owls three.
"Hoot!" said the mother.
"We hoot," said the three.
So they hooted all night
near the hole in the tree.

5

Over in the meadow,
where the grass
grows even,
Lived an old mother cricket
and her little crickets seven.
"Chirp!" said the mother.
"We chirp," said the seven.
So they chirped cheery notes,
In the grass soft and even.

Over in the meadow,
Where the stream runs blue,
Lived a large mother fish
and her little fishes two.
"Swim!" said the mother.
"We swim," said the two.
So they swam all day,
Where the stream runs blue.

Over in the meadow,
by the old green gate.
Lived an old mother duck
and her little ducklings eight.
"Quack!" said the mother.
"We quack," said the eight.
So they quacked in the sun,
By the old green gate.

Over in the meadow,
in the sun,
Lived an old mother turtle
and her little turtle one.
"Dig!" said the mother.
"I dig," said the one.
So they dug, then they rested
In the sand, in the sun.

Over in the meadow,
  where the clear pools shine,
Lived a green mother frog
  and her little froggies nine.
"Jump!" said the mother.
"We jump," said the nine.
So they jumped and they croaked,
  Where the clear pools shine.

18

O ver in the meadow,
    in a cool shady glen,
Lived a mother firefly
    and her little flies ten.
"Shine!" said the mother.
"We shine," said the ten.
So they shone and flew,
In the cool, shady glen.

# Over in the Meadow
based on a traditional rhyme credited to
Olive A. Wadsworth